How to Become an Influencer

A Guide for Beginners and Their Parents

Ruby Galvez

To my siblings Carlo, Melissa, and JP, who
inspire me with their strength.

*"To influence others, walk beside them
rather than in front of them."*
Albert Einstein

TABLE OF CONTENTS

Introduction

Hey there, future superstars! Welcome to a journey that's going to be nothing short of fascinating. Imagine a world where you can turn your hobbies, interests, and even your daily life into something that others enjoy watching and can help you earn some cool cash.

What's the Buzz All About?

So, what's an influencer? An influencer is someone who has the power to affect the decisions of others because of their authority, knowledge, or relationship with their audience. Think of them as the cool people in the digital playground, but instead of just being popular in school, they're popular on the internet.

And guess what? This isn't just for celebrities or people with millions of followers. Anyone with a passion and a unique voice can become an influencer. That is, people willing to put themselves out there for the world to see, literally! But camera-shy people need not worry. There are many strategies to become an influencer even without showing your face, as you'll learn later on.

Let's hop into our time machine for a quick history lesson. Don't worry; there won't be a quiz afterward!

The Roots of Influence: Town Criers, Pamphleteers, and Royal Endorsements

Ah, the good old days! Let's take a stroll down memory lane and explore how influencing has been around for ages, just in different forms. The idea of influencing people's opinions or actions isn't something that popped up with the internet. Oh no, it's as old as human civilization itself! So, let's dig into some of these historical influencers, shall we?

Town Criers: The Original News Feed

Picture a bustling marketplace in a medieval town. People are haggling over fruits or fabrics. Then, you hear a loud bell and a booming voice shouting, "Hear ye, hear ye!" That's the town crier. These folks were the original broadcasters; human news feeds if you will. Dressed in elaborate costumes and carrying a bell, they would walk through the town announcing news, proclamations, or even advertising local businesses. They were the influencers of their time, because people listened to them. Moreover, people trusted the information they shared.

Pamphleteers: The Bloggers of Yesteryears

Pamphleteers were the bloggers of the olden centuries, starting from the time the printing press was invented. These were individuals who wrote short pamphlets about political issues, social commentary, or even scientific discoveries. They'd distribute these pamphlets in public spaces or sell them for a small fee. Some of these pamphlets played a significant role in shaping public opinion, much like how a viral blog post or video can today.

Royal Endorsements: The Ultimate Seal of Approval

Now, let's talk about the crème de la crème of historical influencing: royal endorsements. Imagine you're a merchant selling a commodity, like tea. If the any member of the royalty likes your tea, they might give you a "royal warrant," a seal of approval that you can display proudly. This was a big deal! A royal endorsement was like getting a shout out from the most popular person in the world. It instantly elevated the status of the product and made it highly desirable.

So, the concept of influencing has deep historical roots. The mediums have changed—from town squares to printed pages to digital screens—but the essence remains the same.

Influencing is about connecting with people, sharing valuable information, and sometimes, guiding choices.

Isn't it fascinating to see how far we've come? And now, you're part of this rich fabric of influence. You can add your unique thread to the ever-expanding design.

20th Century Influencers

Fast forward to the 20th century, and we had

movie stars endorsing products on TV. Picture this: you're sitting in your living room watching, and your favorite movie is interrupted by a commercial. There's your favorite movie star, holding up a bottle of soda or a new toy, telling you it's the best ever. That was the power of endorsements back then. These stars were like the kings and queens, and whatever they said was golden.

But the game changed with the coming of the internet and social media. Suddenly, you don't need to be a Hollywood star or a world-class athlete to have a voice. All you need is a smartphone, a dash of creativity, and a sprinkle of charisma. Modern influencers also have the power to affect the decisions of others because of their authority, knowledge, or relationship with their audience.

The Digital Playground

The internet is a vast playground with different corners and spaces where you can hang out. You've got video platforms where you can showcase your talent, be it singing, dancing, or even solving complex math problems. There are picture-sharing platforms where your photography skills can shine. Let's not forget the blogs and websites where your written words can captivate an audience. The best part? You get to choose your playground and the games you want to play!

Not Just Fun and Games

Now, this all sounds like a lot of fun, but is it just

about posting pictures and videos? Nope, there's more to it! Being an influencer can be a real job, and like any job, it comes with responsibilities.

You're not just sharing content; you're building a community. You're creating a space where people come to learn, get inspired, and sometimes, just to have a good laugh.

And yes, you can earn money, but we'll dive deep into that in the upcoming chapters.

The Sky's the Limit

The beauty of being an influencer is that the sky's the limit. Whether you're into cooking, fashion, science experiments, or even collecting rare stamps, there's an audience out there for you.

This isn't just a journey for the tech-savvy people who are already popular. It's a journey for everyone. It's for the quiet person who loves to read and wants to share book reviews. It's for the aspiring chef who can whip up a mean batch of cookies. It's for the parent who's juggling work and wants to share tips on time management.

And yes, it's for the student who's acing their exams and wants to help others do the same.

What's in Store?

So, what can you expect from this guide? We're going to explore the different types of influencers, the various ways you can earn money, and the strategies to maximize your earnings. We'll also delve into the pitfalls to avoid and how to sustain your influence in the long run. I will also be sharing some juicy case studies and real-life examples that you won't want to miss.

Plus, I'm adding done-for-you content plans with scripts for videos, so you can start right away!

Let's Get Started!

Alright, enough chit-chat. Buckle up, because we're about to embark on an incredible adventure. So, turn the page, swipe right, or click next—however you're reading this—and let's dive in!

CHAPTER 1: TYPES OF INFLUENCERS

Micro-Influencers: The Grassroots Movement

Hey there, aspiring influencers! We're diving into a topic that's super relevant and incredibly exciting: micro-Influencers. Now, you might be thinking, "Micro? That sounds small!" But don't let the name fool you. When it comes to impact, these folks are anything but small potatoes. Let's dig in!

Understanding "Micro"

First things first, what does "micro" even mean? In the influencer world, "micro" doesn't mean insignificant; it means focused and specialized. Think of it like this: If the influencer landscape were a big, bustling city, micro-influencers would be the charming neighborhoods that give the city its unique character. They may not have the skyscrapers and flashy billboards, but they've got the cozy cafes, the friendly neighbors, and the local charm that make you feel right at home.

The Numbers Game: Not Just About Followers

One of the coolest things about being a micro-influencer is that you don't need a gazillion followers to make a splash. We're talking anywhere from a few hundred to a few tens of thousands of followers. But here's the kicker. These followers are super engaged! They're not just passive scrollers; they're active participants who listen, comment, and most importantly, trust the influencer. It's like having a classroom where everyone is eager to participate, not just sit in the back and doodle.

The Grassroots Movement: Authenticity is Key

Why do we call it a "grassroots movement"? In politics and social causes, a grassroots movement starts at the local or community level. It's genuine, it's organic, and it's driven by people, not corporations or big organizations. Micro-influencers are the grassroots movement of the digital age. They build their communities from the ground up, and their authenticity shines through. It's like your best friend recommending your favorite book; you're more likely to read it because you trust their opinion.

The Power of Niche: Specialization for the Win

One of the secret sauces that make micro-influencers so effective is their focus on a specific niche. Whether it's vegan cooking, sustainable fashion, or competitive studying (yes, that's my thing!), these influencers are experts in their fields.

They're the go-to sources for tips, reviews, and advice. Imagine having a math whiz in your class who can make even calculus seem like a piece of cake —that's the kind of authority and reliability we're talking about!

The Parental Perspective: Why This Matters for Parents

Now, for the parents in the room, you might be wondering, "Why should I care?"

Well, the micro-influencer route can be a fantastic way for young adults to explore their passions responsibly and constructively. They can learn valuable life skills like communication, community building, and even some business basics—all while focusing on topics they genuinely care about.

Learning by Doing

For the young minds eager to dive in, being a micro-influencer offers a unique learning experience. You're not just absorbing information; you're applying it to real-world scenarios. It's like a hands-on class project that goes beyond the classroom, offering lessons that will serve you well in life.

The Takeaway: Small but Mighty

Micro-influencers may be "small" in terms of follower count, but they're mighty in influence, authenticity, and impact. They're the unsung heroes of the digital world, proving that you don't need to be famous to make a difference.

Ready to join the grassroots movement and become a micro-influencer? It's a journey worth embarking on.

Macro-influencers: The Superstars

Let's dive into the glitzy, glamorous world of macro-influencers. If micro-influencers are the charming neighborhoods of our influencer city, then macro-influencers are the dazzling downtown skyscrapers that light up the skyline. Intrigued? Let's explore!

What Makes a Macro-influencer?

First off, what exactly is a macro-influencer? These are the folks who have follower counts that soar into the hundreds of thousands, millions, or even tens of millions. Imagine a stadium filled with adoring fans—that's the kind of audience we're talking about! But it's not just about the numbers; it's about the wide-reaching impact they have. When a macro-influencer speaks (or posts), the world listens.

Star Power in Action

You know how movie stars and famous athletes have this aura of invincibility around them? That's what we call the "celebrity effect," and macro-influencers have it in spades.

When they recommend a product, share a life tip, or even talk about their favorite books, it's like getting advice from a superstar. It's not just another opinion; it's a headline-making statement.

A Platform for Change

One of the most incredible things about being a macro-influencer is the platform it provides. These influencers have the power to not just sell products but also to inspire change, raise awareness, and even influence public opinion. It's like being the class president with a megaphone that reaches not just your school but schools across the country!

Big Deals and Bigger Responsibilities

Now, let's talk about the business side of things. macro-influencers often have entire teams behind them, managing everything from content creation to brand partnerships. And yes, the earning potential is sky-high.

However, these influencers need to be extra careful about the brands they associate with and the messages they send, as their words can have far-reaching consequences. The failure of their brand to deliver could also mean the influencer's downfall, and vice versa.

The Double-edged Sword

Macro-influencer business can be exciting. On one hand, it offers the chance to turn your passions into a full-fledged career. On the other hand, the spotlight can be intense, and the stakes are high. It's crucial to obtain guidance and support to deal with the complexities of fame and influence.

Dream Big but Stay Grounded

For stars-in-the-making, the path to becoming a macro-influencer may seem like a dream come true.

And it can be! But it's essential to stay grounded. Remember, influence is not just about popularity; it's about making a positive impact. Keep your values intact, and don't lose sight of who you are.

Thought Leaders: The Intellectuals

Let's dive into a category of influencers that's a bit different from the rest. These are the thought leaders, the intellectuals of the influencer world. If macro-influencers are the skyscrapers and micro-influencers are the charming neighborhoods, then thought leaders are the esteemed universities and research centers of our influencer city. Intrigued? Let's dig deeper!

Who are Thought Leaders?

So, what makes someone a thought leader? Well, these are individuals who are experts in their fields, whether it's technology, politics, science, or even lifestyle topics like wellness and sustainability. They're not just sharing selfies or product reviews; they're sharing insights, knowledge, and thought-provoking ideas. Imagine that super-smart teacher who doesn't just follow the textbook but brings in all sorts of cool facts and perspectives—that's a thought leader for you!

The Intellectual Capital: Knowledge is Power

Thought leaders are like walking, talking treasure troves of information. They've got the intellectual capital—valuable knowledge—and they're not afraid to share it. Whether it's through blogs, podcasts, or social media posts, they disseminate information that educates, enlightens, and sometimes even challenges the status quo. Listening to them and scrolling through their content would feel like attending a masterclass.

The Ripple Effect: Influencing the Influencers

One of the most fascinating things about thought leaders is their ability to influence other influencers.

Their ideas are so impactful that they often set the tone for discussions and debates in their respective fields. It's like being the trendsetter in your school; once you start something, everyone else wants to join in.

The Responsibility: Credibility and Ethics

Being a thought leader comes with a heavy responsibility. These influencers need to ensure that their information is accurate, unbiased, and ethical.

Misinformation can spread like wildfire. Thought leaders have the duty to be the firefighters, not the arsonists.

They lead fact-checking quests and aren't shy about calling out people who twist facts.

For parents, this means teaching young influencers the importance of fact-checking and ethical conduct, especially if they aspire to be thought leaders.

A Pathway to Lifelong Learning

For the young minds out there, aspiring to be a

thought leader is like signing up for a lifetime of learning. It's not just about gaining followers; it's about expanding your horizons, diving deep into subjects you're passionate about, and becoming an authority in your field. It's like taking your favorite subject in school and turning it into a lifelong project.

The Thinkers of Tomorrow

So, what's the big takeaway? Thought leaders are the intellectuals who enrich the influencer landscape with depth, wisdom, and credibility. They're the thinkers of tomorrow, shaping not just opinions but also the very fabric of our knowledge.

Activist influencers: The Change Makers

Let's dive into a truly inspiring category of influencers: the activist influencers. These are the folks who use their platforms not just for likes and shares, but for meaningful change. If our influencer city has skyscrapers, neighborhoods, and universities, then activist influencers are the passionate community organizers and the rallying protesters. Ready to be inspired? Let's go!

The Heart of the Matter

First up, what makes an activist influencer? Well, these are the individuals who are deeply committed to a cause, whether it's social justice, environmental conservation, mental health awareness, or any other issue that needs attention. They're not just talking the talk; they're walking the walk.

Imagine that one student in class who not only recycles but also educates everyone about reducing waste—that's an activist influencer for you!

Amplifying Voices

One of the most powerful tools an activist influencer has is their platform. They use it like a megaphone to amplify voices that might otherwise go unheard. Whether it's sharing stories, spreading petitions, or organizing virtual rallies, these influencers know how to mobilize their audience. It's like being the captain of a team; you're not just playing well yourself, but you're also encouraging everyone else to give their best.

The Ripple of Change: Impact Beyond the Screen

What sets activist influencers apart is the tangible impact they make. They're not just influencing opinions; they're influencing actions. Whether it's raising funds for a charity, driving policy change, or simply educating the masses, the ripple effect of their work often extends far beyond the digital world. It's like planting a tree; the benefits are long-lasting and reach far and wide.

The Weight of Responsibility: Ethics and Authenticity

Being an activist influencer is a big responsibility. These influencers have to be incredibly careful about the information they share and the causes they support. Authenticity and credibility are key. For parents, this is a great opportunity to teach young influencers about the importance of due diligence and ethical responsibility. It's not just about what you stand for, but also how you stand for it.

Young Activists in the Making

For the young activists among us, this path offers an incredible learning journey. You'll learn not just about the issues you care about, but also about how to communicate effectively, how to research thoroughly, and how to inspire action. It's like a real-world course in leadership, ethics, and social studies all rolled into one!

The Takeaway: Be the Change You Wish to See

So, what's the big takeaway? Activist influencers are the change-makers of the digital world. They show us that influence isn't just about popularity; it's about purpose. They remind us that social media can be a force for good, turning hashtags into movements and likes into meaningful action.

Whether you're a parent nurturing a young activist or a student eager to make a difference, the path of an activist influencer is both challenging and rewarding.

Ready to raise your voice and be the change you wish to see in the world? Let's turn that passion into action, future activist influencers!

The Hybrid: Wearing Multiple Hats

Let's dive into a fascinating and versatile category of influencers: the hybrids. These are the multi-talented folks who don't fit neatly into just one box. They're the Renaissance men and women of the digital age, dabbling in various fields and excelling in more than one. If our influencer city has skyscrapers, neighborhoods, universities, and community organizers, then the hybrids are the multi-purpose complexes that house a bit of everything. Intrigued? Let's explore!

The Jack-of-All-Trades

So, what's a hybrid influencer? Imagine someone who's not just a fashion guru but also a tech whiz. Or someone who's both a fitness enthusiast and a passionate advocate for mental health.

These influencers are like the students who excel in both sports and academics; they're well-rounded and multi-faceted. They bring a unique blend of skills and interests to the table, making them incredibly relatable to a wide range of audiences.

Mastering Multiple Roles

Being a hybrid influencer is like being a juggler; you've got multiple balls in the air, and you've got to keep them all going. It's a balancing act that requires planning, time management, and a whole lot of energy. But the payoff is huge. You get to explore different facets of your personality and share a richer, more diverse range of content. It's like being the lead in a school play while also being the star of the soccer team—challenging but oh-so-rewarding!

The Synergy Effect

One of the best things about being a hybrid is the "Synergy Effect." That's when two different areas of expertise come together to create something even more amazing.

For example, a hybrid who's into both cooking and sustainability can create content that not only tantalizes the taste buds but also saves the planet. It's like combining math and art to create the most amazing geometric designs; the whole is greater than the sum of its parts.

Navigating Multiple Identities

Being a hybrid isn't all sunshine and rainbows. It comes with its own set of challenges, like maintaining authenticity while navigating multiple identities.

For parents, this means helping young influencers find a harmonious balance between their various interests. It's like helping them prepare for both the science fair and the talent show; each requires a different set of skills and a different version of them.

The Ultimate Learning Experience

For the young and ambitious, being a hybrid offers

the ultimate learning experience. You're not just honing one skill; you're developing multiple talents. You're learning how to adapt, how to switch gears, and how to integrate different parts of yourself into one cohesive brand. It's like taking a cross-disciplinary course that prepares you for the complexities of the real world.

The Future is Hybrid

So, what's the big takeaway? Hybrid influencers are the future. They show us that you don't have to limit yourself to one path; you can explore multiple avenues and still find success. They embody the spirit of adaptability and versatility, essential skills in our ever-changing digital landscape.

Whether you're a parent guiding a multi-talented prodigy or a young adult influencer with diverse passions, the hybrid path is an exciting and fulfilling journey.

CHAPTER 2: HOW TO EARN

Hello, future moguls! Buckle up, because we're diving into a topic that's on everyone's mind: making money, or as we like to call it, the art of monetization. If the influencer world is a bustling marketplace, then this chapter is your guide to setting up the most fabulous stall. Intrigued? Let's get down to business!

The Currency of Influence: More Than Just Dollars and Cents

First things first, let's talk about what "monetization" actually means. In the simplest terms, it's the process of turning your influence into income. But hold on a minute; it's not just about raking in the cash. It's about building a sustainable model that rewards your creativity, expertise, and, most importantly, your connection with your audience. Sustainable means you can continue doing it for a long time with minimal resource depletion.

Diversify Revenue Streams!

Now, let's talk about the various ways you can monetize your influence. There's a smorgasbord of options out there, and the key is to diversify. Here's a quick rundown:

Ads: Think of these as the billboards of your digital highway. They're a straightforward way to earn, but they require a large and engaged audience.

Sponsorships: This is like having a patron for your art. Brands pay you to promote their products!

Affiliate Marketing: Here, you're the middleman. You promote a product and get a commission for every sale made through your unique link.

Merchandising: Got a catchy slogan or a cool logo? Turn it into merchandise like t-shirts, mugs, or even eBooks.

Accepting Stars/Tips: This is your virtual tip jar. Your audience can show their appreciation by sending you small payments, often during live streams.

Subscriptions: This is for the die-hard fans. Offer exclusive content for a monthly fee, creating a steady income stream.

The Strategy Game: Playing Your Cards Right

Monetization isn't just about choosing a revenue stream; it's about strategizing how to make the most of it. For example, if you're going the sponsorship route, you'll need to think about how to integrate the product seamlessly into your content. Or if you're selling merchandise, you'll need to consider production costs, shipping, and customer service. It's like a game of chess; every move needs to be calculated.

The Ethical Angle: Responsibility and Transparency

Here's something super important: ethics. Monetization comes with a responsibility to be transparent with your audience. If you're promoting a product, disclose that it's a sponsored post. If you're offering affiliate links, make that clear. In fact, many platforms require that their users disclose their monetization status.

For parents, this is a golden opportunity to teach young adults about the importance of honesty and integrity in business.

A Lesson in Real-World Business

For the young influencers out there, monetization is like a real-world business class. You'll learn about marketing, finance, customer relations, and so much more. And the best part? You'll earn while you learn!

Monetization as a Journey, Not a Destination

So, what's the big takeaway? Monetization is not a one-time event; it's a journey. It's about building a business model that aligns with your brand, values, and audience. It's about turning your passion into a profession, and your influence into a sustainable income.

Whether you're a parent guiding your young influencer through this entrepreneurial adventure, or a young influencer eager to monetize your platform, this chapter is your roadmap to financial success.

Advertisements: The Traditional Route

Often considered the bread and butter of the digital world, ads are the most traditional and straightforward way to monetize your influence. But there's an art to doing it right. So, let's roll up our sleeves and delve into the nitty-gritty of ad placements and revenue sharing.

Understanding Ad Placement

Think of your digital platform—be it a blog, a video channel, or a social media account—as a bustling highway. The advertisements are the billboards along this highway. Where you place these billboards matters a lot. Place them too close together, and you risk overwhelming your audience. Scatter them too far apart, and you miss out on potential revenue. It's a balancing act, much like deciding where to place products in a physical store to catch the customer's eye.

Types of Ad Placements:

Pre-roll and Post-roll ads are the ads that appear before or after your video content. They're like the appetizers and desserts that bookend a main course.

Banner Ads are the ads that appear at the top or bottom of your webpage or within the content. Think of them as the signs you see hanging in a store window.

Interstitial Ads are full-screen ads that appear

between different pages or sections of your content. They're like commercial breaks during a TV show.

Native Ads are ads that blend seamlessly into your content, often looking like another post or article. They're the in-store samples that you might not even realize are promoting a product.

Let's talk about the money! Ad revenue is typically shared between the platform and the content creator—that's you! The exact percentage can vary, but it's crucial to understand how this pie is sliced.

Ad Revenue Sharing Models

Cost Per Mille (CPM)

This model pays you for every thousand views your ad receives. It's like getting a small commission for every thousand people who walk past a billboard you own.

Cost Per Click (CPC)

Here, you get paid every time someone clicks on the ad. Imagine owning a vending machine; you earn money each time someone makes a purchase.

Cost Per Acquisition (CPA)

In this model, you earn when someone not only clicks the ad but also makes a purchase or signs up for a service. It's like being a real estate agent. You get a cut when you successfully close a deal.

Transparency and Relevance

Before we move on, let's touch on ethics. It's crucial to be transparent about the fact that you're earning money from these ads. Most platforms will automatically indicate when a post is sponsored, but it's good practice to remind your audience now and then.

For parents, this is an excellent opportunity to instill the values of honesty and transparency in your budding entrepreneurs.

Moreover, relevance is key. The ads that appear should be relevant to your content and your audience. No one wants to see an ad for lawn mowers in the middle of a beauty tutorial!

A Lesson in Economics and Ethics

For young influencers, this is more than just a way to make money. It's a lesson in economics —supply, demand, pricing strategies—and ethics. You're learning how to provide value to advertisers while maintaining trust with your audience. It's a real-world class in business ethics and economics rolled into one.

Ads as a Stepping Stone

So, what's the big takeaway? Advertisements are often the first step in an influencer's monetization journey. They offer a relatively easy entry point but mastering them requires a blend of strategic thinking, ethical considerations, and audience understanding.

Whether you're a parent helping your young adult navigate this complex landscape, or a young influencer eager to take the first step into monetization, understanding ad placements and revenue sharing is crucial.

Sponsorships: The Brand Partnerships

If advertisements are the billboards along your digital highway, then sponsorships are the high-end boutiques that invite you in for an exclusive experience. Intrigued? Let's explore the ins and outs of these brand partnerships.

A Mutually Beneficial Relationship

At its core, a sponsorship is a partnership between you, the influencer, and a brand. It's like a friendship where both parties bring something valuable to the table.

You offer the brand exposure to your audience, and in return, the brand compensates you, often both financially and with free products or experiences.

It's a win-win, but like any relationship, it requires care, attention, and above all, compatibility. Your audience and own personal brand must be in alignment with your sponsor.

Example, you can't promote adult-targeted products if your audience comprises people of a younger age range.

If you're targeting parents, the products you endorse must be those they are likely to buy.

Types of Sponsorships

Product Reviews

The brand sends you a product, and you review it for

your audience. Think of it as a show-and-tell session where you share your honest opinions. You may be required to use the product yourself.

Sponsored Posts

These are posts that the brand pays you to create, often featuring their product or service. For example, if a colored pencil brand is paying you to talk about them, you can create a video log of your latest art creation. If a spice brand is paying you top dollar to show their products, then host a cooking show.

Long-term Partnerships

These are ongoing relationships where you become a brand ambassador. It's akin to being on a sports team; you wear the jersey, and you represent the team in various competitions. This means being responsible for your image, because the brand's reputation depends on how well you carry yourself in your everyday life.

The Art of Negotiation: Setting Your Worth

Ah, the money talk! This is where things get interesting. How much should you charge for a sponsorship? It's a bit like setting the price for a piece of art; various factors come into play, such as your reach, engagement rate, and the complexity of the content you'll create. Negotiation skills are key here, and for the young influencers, this is a real-world lesson in economics and self-worth.

The Ethical Angle: Authenticity and Disclosure

Sponsorships come with a responsibility to remain authentic and transparent. You owe it to your audience to disclose that you're being compensated for promoting a product or service.

Most platforms have guidelines for this, often requiring you to use tags like #sponsored or #ad. You can also state at the beginning of your post that you were paid to promote the product you will be talking about.

This is an invaluable opportunity to learn about ethical business practices and the importance of honesty.

A Masterclass in Business Relations

Sponsorships offer a masterclass in business relations. You'll learn how to negotiate contracts, how to maintain professional relationships, and how to balance the demands of various stakeholders. It's like a group project where you're not just responsible for your part but also for coordinating with others to create something greater.

Sponsorships as a Career Milestone

So, what's the big picture? Sponsorships are often a significant milestone in an influencer's career. They signify that you've reached a level of influence and credibility that brands are willing to invest in.

Sponsorships require a level of professionalism, transparency, and ethical conduct that sets the stage for your future in the industry.

Whether you're a parent guiding your young influencer through these complex negotiations or a young influencer eager to take this significant step, understanding the dynamics of sponsorships is crucial.

Affiliate Marketing: The Sales Catalyst

Let's dive into a monetization strategy that's as intriguing as it is rewarding: Affiliate Marketing. If sponsorships are the high-end boutiques of your digital world, then affiliate marketing is your bustling marketplace, where transactions happen left and right. Curious to know how you can be the catalyst for these sales? Let's dive in!

What is Affiliate Marketing?

Affiliate marketing is a performance-based monetization model where you earn a commission for driving sales or actions to a brand. Imagine you're the host of a party, and you introduce two friends who hit it off instantly. As a thank-you, they each give you a small gift.

In affiliate marketing, your platform is the party, your audience is one friend, and the brand is the other. When they "hit it off" (i.e., a sale is made), you get a small commission as a thank-you.

Types of Affiliate Marketing

Product Links

These are specific links that you share in your content. When someone clicks and makes a purchase, you earn a commission. It's like recommending a book to a friend; if they buy it, you get a small reward.

Coupon Codes

Brands provide you with a unique coupon code that your audience can use for a discount. Each time the code is used, you earn a commission. Think of it as handing out discount flyers for a local store and getting a cut for every customer who walks in.

Lead Generation

Here, you're rewarded for driving potential customers to a brand's website, where they might sign up for a service or newsletter.

It's like inviting friends to a community event. You're not responsible for what they do there, but you get points (or monetary gain) for bringing them in.

The Strategy: Tailoring Content to Your Audience

The key to successful affiliate marketing is relevance. The products or services you promote must align with your content and resonate with your audience. It's like recommending movies to your friends; you wouldn't suggest a horror flick to someone who loves rom-coms.

Tailoring your affiliate marketing efforts to your audience's interests, including picking products and services that your audience would appreciate, increases the likelihood of conversions, a.k.a. sales or leads, and therefore, your commissions.

Transparency and Trust

Affiliate marketing, like any form of monetization, requires ethical considerations. You must disclose that you'll earn a commission if your audience clicks on an affiliate link or uses your coupon code. Transparency builds trust. Moreover, some platforms require you to disclose.

A Lesson in Sales and Psychology

Affiliate marketing is a practical lesson in sales techniques and consumer psychology. You'll learn how to craft compelling calls to action, how to understand your audience's needs, and how to present products in a way that solves problems or fulfills desires. It's like a mini-MBA program wrapped into your daily influencing activities.

Affiliate Marketing as a Sustainable Model

So, what's the grand takeaway? Affiliate marketing offers a sustainable and scalable way to monetize your influence.

It allows you to earn passive income, meaning you can make money even when you're not actively working. However, it requires a deep understanding of your audience, a strategic approach, and a commitment to ethical practices.

Just to be clear, passive income means you set it up correctly and put all your effort into creating early on. Then, your repertoire of content with affiliate links would do the work for you in the future even

RUBY GALVEZ

when you're no longer working on them.

Merchandising: The Personal Brand Store

Welcome to the world of online marketing, where we're about to unlock the secrets of turning your personal brand into a merchandise powerhouse!

This section is all about creating your own merchandise store that resonates with your audience. We'll keep it friendly, relatable, and, most importantly, profitable.

Why Merchandising Matters

You've built your following, your channel is booming, and your followers adore you. Now, it's time to give them a tangible piece of your world. Merchandising isn't just about selling products; it's about strengthening your connection with your audience.

When they wear or use items branded with your logo or catchphrases, they become walking billboards for your brand. It's a win-win!

Here are the steps to merchandising!

Step 1: Define Your Brand Identity

Before you dive into merchandise creation, take a moment to reflect on your brand's identity. What values, colors, and themes define you? Your merchandise should be an extension of your brand, so make sure it aligns seamlessly.

There must be a slogan or a line that you say in your

videos that your followers love. Write that across your brand shirt or mug!

Step 2: Choose Your Products

Let's get creative with product selection. Think about what resonates with your audience. Are they into apparel, accessories, or perhaps something more unique like custom mugs or phone cases? The key is to offer products that your followers will love to incorporate into their daily lives.

Recommended products for influencers: lanyards, shirts, mugs, pens, stationery, and phone/laptop stickers.

Create designs that reflect your personality and resonate with your audience. Whether it's witty slogans, beautiful artwork, or a combination of both, your designs should scream "you." Consider hiring a designer if needed, but make sure your vision is always at the forefront.

Step 3: Choose a Merchandise Platform

To get your merchandise out there, you'll need a platform to sell it. There are several options, like Print-on-Demand services, eCommerce platforms, or even social media marketplaces. Pick one that aligns with your budget and technical abilities.

Step 4: Set Up Your Store

Time to roll up those sleeves and set up your store!

This involves adding product listings, uploading your designs, and configuring payment and shipping options. Make sure your store looks clean, professional, and user-friendly. Friendly navigation is the name of the game!

Step 5: Promote Your Merchandise

Your store is ready, but now you need to get the word out. Utilize your social media channels, create promotional posts, and engage with your audience to generate hype. Run giveaways, share behind-the-scenes content, and showcase satisfied customers wearing or using your merchandise.

Step 6: Fulfill Orders and Provide Stellar Customer Service

When the orders start rolling in, make sure you have a reliable system for order fulfillment. Ensure that your customers receive their items promptly and in top-notch condition. Excellent customer service will keep them coming back for more.

Pro Tips for Success

1. Start Small: It's okay to begin with a few key products and expand as your brand grows.

2. Quality Matters: Invest in high-quality merchandise that your customers will love and use.

3. Collaborate: Consider collaborating with other influencers or brands to expand your reach.

4. Stay Consistent: Maintain a consistent brand image across all merchandise and marketing efforts.

5. Legalities: Be aware of copyright and trademark laws to avoid any legal issues with your designs.

Creating your personal brand merchandise store is a fantastic way to monetize your online presence and deepen your connection with your audience.

Accepting Stars/Tips: The Fan-Funded Model

We've talked about a lot of stuff already, from what an influencer is to some pretty cool ways to make money online. But guess what? We're diving into another awesome topic: accepting tips and stars from your fans.

Trust me, you don't want to skip this one—it's like the cherry on top of your influencer sundae!

So, let's break it down. You know when you go to a coffee shop and you see that tip jar sitting on the counter?

Well, in the online world, that's kind of like what tips are. Your followers can give you a little extra "thank you" for the cool stuff you post. Except this isn't spare change; we're talking real money here!

Why It's So Cool

What makes the fan-funded model super awesome is that it's really about that direct connection with your audience. They're supporting you, and you feel their support as you're creating content.

You know, those die-hard fans who comment "First!" on all your posts or always share your stuff? Yeah, those peeps can actually send you money as a way of saying, "Hey, you're awesome!"

How Does It Work?

Here's the how-to part. Depending on the platform

you're using there'll be an option to set up some kind of tipping feature.

The point is, once you set this up, your fans can start tipping you as you do your livestream or while playing your reels. Cha-ching!

Why Would People Tip Me?

Great question! Here's the deal. People aren't just going to throw money at you because you asked nicely (though it'd be super cool if life worked that way, huh?).

The idea is to give your audience something they can't resist. Maybe you're a gamer who does hilarious live streams. Or perhaps you're a DIYer who makes complicated stuff seem easy. If you provide value—like, real, "I got to try that!" value—people will want to thank you for it. And what better way to thank you than with a tip?

Are There Rules?

Yes, there are rules. First off, you've got to be clear that tips are not mandatory. Your content is still free for anyone to enjoy, and tipping is just a bonus for you.
Also, depending on the platform, there may be age restrictions or other guidelines you've got to follow. You don't want to break any rules and lose out on this cool money-making opportunity, right?

The Do's and Don'ts

Let's get some quick tips going. For the Do's:

- Do make your tipping feature easy to find.
- Do thank people who tip you, either by shoutout or some other cool way.
- Do keep giving quality content; that's why people are tipping you in the first place!

For the Don'ts:

- Don't beg for tips; nobody likes that.
- Don't ignore your fans who can't afford to tip; they're still awesome and help grow your brand.
- Don't let the tips change the kind of content you create. Stay true to you!

The Real Deal

Alright, guys, let's get real for a sec. The fan-funded model won't turn you into a millionaire overnight. But it's one more way to show that what you're doing matters. Plus, it's super gratifying to know that someone liked your content enough to give you their hard-earned money.

Subscriptions: The Exclusive Club

Let's dig into something that's like having a VIP section for your online club: subscriptions. It's like getting an exclusive backstage pass to your favorite concert.

The VIP Experience, Online-Style

So, what's the subscription model all about? Picture this: you've got a special club where only the coolest of the cool can hang out.

These subscribers get extra perks, like secret handshakes, private Q&As, and even some behind-the-scenes action.

But, what's the catch? They have to pay a monthly or yearly fee to keep their VIP status.

Why Subscriptions Rock

Okay, so why is this subscription thing so neat? First off, it's predictable money. Unlike ad revenue, which can go up and down faster than a roller coaster, subscriptions give you a steady income because they renew monthly unless the users cancel.

It's like knowing you'll always have fries to go with that burger—comforting, right?

Setting Up Your Exclusive Club

Most social media platforms offer some kind of subscription service. Even some blogging platforms let you put content behind a paywall. The trick is to make sure you're offering something that's worth the price of admission.

What's in It for Them?

Why would someone want to subscribe? Think about it: they're already getting your regular content for free, so what's the special sauce?

Maybe you offer exclusive videos or articles that only subscribers can access. Perhaps you do special live streams where you answer their burning questions. Or maybe you release new stuff early just for them.

Whatever it is, make it so awesome that people can't help but want in.

Some Ground Rules

Yes, there are always rules. You have to make sure what you're offering is within the guidelines of whatever platform you're using.

Be real with your fans. Let them know what they can expect when they subscribe, and don't promise things you can't deliver. That's like promising your friends a pizza party and then showing up with a single slice—not cool.

Do's and Don'ts, VIP Edition

- Do offer real value that makes the subscription worth it.
- Do engage with your subscribers. They're

your VIPs, so make them feel special.
- Do be transparent about what the subscription includes.

- Don't neglect your non-subscribers. You're still an influencer for everyone, not just the VIPs.
- Don't lock all your content behind a paywall. Keep some goodies for your general audience.
- Don't forget to give your subscribers a shout-out now and then; they love that recognition!

The Real Talk

Look, setting up a subscription service isn't a guarantee you'll be rolling in dough. But, it's a cool way to connect with your most committed fans while making some extra cash.

CHAPTER 3: STRATEGIES TO MAXIMIZE EARNINGS

The Long and Short Videos: A Comparative Analysis

Now let's tackle another hot topic that's probably been buzzing around in your head: long videos versus short videos. Which one brings in more cash? What are the ups and downs of each? Grab some popcorn, because we're diving right in!

Long vs. Short

In one corner, we've got long videos: these are your 10-minute-plus deep dives, how-to's, and let's-plays. In the other corner, we've got short videos that are seldom longer than one minute.

Earning Potential

Long Video Pros:

- More Ad Revenue: Longer videos mean more opportunities for ad placements.
- Depth: You can go deep into a subject,

building a more intimate relationship with your audience.

- Viewer Engagement: The longer someone watches, the more platforms reward you with exposure, not to mention more tips from viewers for live feeds.

Long Video Cons:

- Time-Consuming: Producing long-form content can take a lot of time, and let's be real, time is money.
- Risk of Boredom: Keep it engaging, or you might lose viewers—and money.

Short Video Pros:

- Quick and Easy: These videos are generally easier to make, meaning you can churn out a lot more content.
- Viral Potential: Short videos are more shareable, which could mean a ton of new eyeballs on you.
- Engagement: They're quick, catchy, and people are more likely to watch the whole thing.

Short Video Cons:

- Limited Ad Revenue: Not much room for multiple ads here.
- Shallow Engagement: You get less time to connect with your viewers.

What Works for You?

Ask yourself: what's your style? Are you the type to sit down and talk for an hour, or do you like quick, snappy updates? Your personal vibe is a huge factor in what will work best for you.

Why Not Both?

Now, here's the kicker: who says you have to choose? Some creators use short videos to lure folks in and long videos to keep them around. It's like using a teaser trailer to get people excited about a full-length movie.

The Real Deal

In the end, both types of videos have their pros and cons when it comes to earning potential. Long videos require a time investment, but they are satisfying. Short videos are like snacks; you need a lot of them to feel full.

Your best bet might be to mix it up. Give your audience a taste of both worlds, and you might just maximize your earnings while keeping things fresh and exciting.

Websites and Blogs

Today, we're throwing it back and talking about something that might seem a little old-school but is still super relevant: websites and blogs. Grab a comfy seat because this one is full of hidden gems!

Blogging: A Blast from the Past

First off, what's the deal with blogging? Didn't that peak like, a decade ago? Well, yes and no. Blogs have been around since the late '90s. They started as digital diaries, transformed into journalistic platforms, and then exploded into a mix of everything—from food recipes to tech reviews.

Here's the kicker: people are still reading blogs, and you can still make serious cash from them. So, if you think blogs are outdated, think again!

Earning Potential

Just like videos, blogs can make money through ads, sponsored posts, affiliate marketing, and merchandising. Plus, you can also turn your blog into a membership site.

Everything you can do on different platforms, you can do on a website and a domain name you own (or technically, renting from a domain name server).

The Safety Net

You know how you can get grounded for breaking house rules? Well, social media and other ecommerce platforms are kind of like that. If you violate their guidelines—even accidentally—your account could get banned or demonetized. Poof! There goes your audience and income.

Owning a website or blog is like having your own place. You set the rules. So even if you get kicked off YouTube or Instagram, you still have your website where your fans can find you and you can still make money.

The Do's for Websites and Blogs:
- Do make your site user-friendly. No one likes clunky websites and those that don't translate well to mobile users.
- Do provide valuable content that people actually want to read.
- Do engage with your audience through comments, emails, or newsletters.

The Don'ts:
- Don't spam your readers with too many ads
- Don't plagiarize content; that's not only illegal but also uncool.
- Don't ignore Search Engine Optimization; it's your best friend for getting more eyeballs on your site.

Social Media: The Community Builder

Let's get into something super crucial: social media. Believe it or not, social media is like the glue that holds all your money-making pieces together. Let's dive into why it's such a big deal, how it started, and how it can pad your pockets!

Earning Potential

You're probably wondering, "How can tweets turn into cash?" Great question, and the answer is simpler than you'd think.

Sponsored Posts

Brands will actually pay you to post about their stuff. The more followers you have, the bigger the paycheck.

Merch Sales

Got a cool slogan or design? Slap that baby on a t-shirt and promote it on your social media. Your followers are your first customers!

Fan Interaction

Social media is where you tell your fans about subscriptions you're running and new projects!

Affiliate Marketing

You can promote products and get a cut when your followers buy something through your special link.

The key to unlocking this treasure chest is growing a community of loyal fans. The bigger and more engaged your community, the more ways you can earn.

Why You Need to be Social

Imagine you're throwing the most awesome party ever, but you forget to send out invites. That's what it's like to try making money online without social media—you're missing out on letting a ton of people know how awesome you are!

- Credibility: Having a strong social media presence can make you look legit. It's like a street cred for the Internet.

- Exposure: More followers mean more visibility.

- Community: Your social media fans aren't just dollar signs; they're your community. They'll give you feedback, share your content, and even defend you against Internet trolls.

The "Invisible" Influencer

What if I told you there's a way to be an influencer without ever showing your face? Mind-blowing, right? Buckle up, because we're diving into the fascinating world of the "Invisible" Influencer, also known as "Faceless."

Who Are These Mysterious Figures?

"Invisible" Influencers are ninjas of sorts. They may never show their faces, but you definitely know their work.

Some works done by these folks are those awesome how-to videos, animation channels, and voice-over travel guides that get millions of views on video-sharing platforms. You never see them, but you're definitely familiar with their unique style or voice.

Earning Potential of a "Faceless" Channel

Being invisible doesn't mean you're missing out on the money train. Here's how you can cash in:

1. Sponsorships: Even without showing your face, you can partner with brands that align with your content. For example, if you run a cooking channel, get affiliate links for kitchenware brands.

2. Ads: Your videos can still get tons of views, which means ad money still rolls

in. Also, platforms don't care if you show your face; they care if people watch!

3. Affiliate Marketing: Doing a how-to video on crafting? Drop an affiliate link for the materials you are using in your description box.

4. Product Sales: You can still have branded merch as a faceless channel. For example, sell custom sketches if you run an art tutorial channel!

Why Go Invisible?

You might wonder why anyone would choose to be an invisible influencer. Well, there are a few reasons:

- Privacy: You keep your identity a secret, which can be a big plus for a lot of people.

- Lower Production Costs: You don't need a top-of-the-line camera, lighting, or even a glam squad. Your content is the star.

- Focus on Skills: People will follow you for your skills, knowledge, or the stories you tell, not for what you look like or what you're wearing.

CHAPTER 4: NICHES

Choosing a niche is like choosing a life partner; go with something you love, something you can commit to, and something that makes the hard work feel like a breeze.

If you've ever wondered, "What should I make videos about?" or "What should I blog or tweet?" then you're not yet set on one niche.

You can go for niches with underserved audiences. You can also put your unique twist on a popular niche.

To find your niche, consider these three big sections: Passion and Interests, Success Stories, and what's on the horizon—Emerging Trends.

Passion and Interest

When I say passion, I mean the "I-could-talk-about-this-all-day" kind. Why? Because if you love what you're doing, it won't feel like work. Also, you can create thousands of videos about something you really like.

Imagine you're a total geek for books, like me.

You love the history, you love the rarity, and you love the nostalgia of seeing books that trended in yesteryears. If you start a channel or a blog around a passion, not only do you get to enjoy your hobby even more, but you'll also come across as authentic.

This passion can translate into cash! Once you've gathered a community that trusts you, they're more likely to follow your recommendations, buy your merch, or even directly support you with tips or subscriptions.

Success Stories

Now let's get into some real-world examples of influencers who took the path less traveled and hit the jackpot.

An Influencer Who Loves Indoor Plants

There is a channel of a person who's mad about houseplants. They have all this content about how not to kill your indoor plants. Apparently, so many other people could relate to their content, and so, they attract so many followers. Sponsorships from gardening brands, their own plant-care guide books, and a super-loyal community.

The Food Gobblers

This one's wild. Creators are making videos of themselves eating crunchy foods next to a high-quality microphone, and so many people are tuning in! Audio art, some people call it. But it's really just enjoying your food and letting people in on how crunchy it is. Some food channels like these are faceless, just the sound is heard. People go crazy over it!

Virtual Travel Guides

During the pandemic, people started exploring virtual video game worlds and giving travel-style commentary. Influencers who did this are raking in money from game companies who want them to feature their virtual worlds.

Emerging Trends

What niches might be the next big thing? Here are some ideas.

VR and AR (Virtual and Augmented Realities)

As technology gets better, VR and AR are becoming more mainstream. Influencers who use these technologies would likely stand out.

Mental Health and Mindfulness

Modern life leads to various stresses, and even just standing in line or being stuck in traffic can make people feel tense. Influencers can help people seek ways to stay grounded.
Mindfulness apps, guided meditations, or even online counseling niches could be huge.

Personal Finance for Youth

The term adulting has gone mainstream, and its being coined only means young people are finding it difficult to cope with finances. Finance gurus or even just folks who are good with handling money can help these young people thrive.

Help them understand taxes, investing, and budgeting and you have yourself an avid audience. If you're good with money, this could be a goldmine.

Sustainability and Eco-Friendly Living

Everything points to climate change, which has become a hot topic. Eco-friendly hacks or sustainable living systems you developed yourself can become gold mines.

64

Content Calendars: Planning for Success

Here is your cheat sheet for never running out of cool stuff to talk about throughout the year. Ready? Let's go!

Monthly Content Ideas

Synchronizing your content with holidays and specific events can maximize your earnings because people would want to participate and would likely celebrate the same holidays.

January: New Year, Martin Luther King Jr. Day
February: Valentine's Day, Presidents' Day
March: Spring, St. Patrick's Day
April: Spring, Easter, Earth Day
May: Mother's Day, Memorial Day
June: Schools Out, Flag Day, Father's Day
July: Independence Day
August: Summer
September: Back to School, Labor Day
October: Halloween
November: Thanksgiving, Veterans Day
December: Christmas, Hanukkah, Kwanzaa

Weekly and Daily Content Ideas

Here's a sample weekly content calendar that focuses on consistent events.

Motivated Monday: Share an inspiring quote or story on all your social media platforms to get people pumped for the week. Keep the music upbeat, because we're setting the tone for the week.

Tuesday Tutorials: A video describing steps on how to do something can drag in all the good views. You can also do a review or an analysis.

Witty Wednesday: Share a quote or a mantra. Have a small talk session talking about your projects behind the scenes. This would humanize you and make your audience feel part of your process.

Throwback Thursday: Share a favorite old video, a toy from your childhood, a vintage piece in your home, or even a look back at how far you've come. You can get extra mileage from past content and old items that you've been keeping.

Fan Friday: You can do shout-outs to followers during your live. You can also answer fan questions!

Share-worthy Saturday: Do bigger events on Saturdays, like a contest, a poll, or a game. Your followers can engage longer with your content because it's Saturday. You can gather insight into what your audience likes and dislikes.

Sun Day Sunday: You can do a vlog of yourself enjoying a local park or attraction.

Tips

1. Shoot many videos in one batch: It's easier to shoot three videos in one go than to set everything up three separate times.

2. Automation: Use tools that allow you to schedule social media and blog posts in advance.

3. Track and Tweak: After you've run this schedule for a few weeks, check your stats. See what's working and what needs more work.

CHAPTER 5: INFLUENCER ISSUES

Can you believe we're at the end of this rollercoaster ride? Time flies when you're spilling the tea on all things influencer-related, right? But wait; some not-so-glamorous issues still need to be discussed.

Burnout

When influencing feels like work, you're tired, uninspired, and even the thought of picking up a camera feels like lifting a boulder. Not even the prospect of making money excites you anymore.

Solutions:

1. Take a break. Your true fans will understand.
2. Outsource. Hire someone for tasks that drain you.
3. Re-evaluate: Modify your niche or schedule.

Trolls

Trolls are the cockroaches of the internet. They get a kick out of bringing influencers down. While it's tough and it would be more gratifying to tell them off, don't feed the trolls. Engaging with them would make them even more excited.

Solutions:

1. Moderate Comments: Many platforms allow you to filter comments based on keywords.
2. Ignore: Most trolls move on if they don't get the reaction they're seeking.
3. Block and Report: Use the tools available on platforms to make your space safer.

Banned

Each platform has its own set of rules. Violating them could get you banned.

Solutions:

1. Read the fine print
2. Stay updated on policy changes
3. Have a backup plan, like another site where your fans can interact with you.

Cancel Culture

One wrong tweet from a decade ago can resurface and, before you know it, #Cancel[YourNameHere] is trending.

Solutions:

1. Be Mindful: Think before you post.
2. Apologize: If you mess up, own it.
3. Learn and Improve

Parental Perspective for Guiding Young Influencers

Your young influencers might be digital natives, but they need your wisdom. Guide them in choosing a niche that's appropriate and help them understand that it's not all fun and games.

School and other responsibilities are crucial, no arguments there. Help your young influencer set a schedule that accommodates both their education and their online activities.

Discuss the importance of honesty, especially when it comes to sponsored content. Teach them about the responsibilities that come with influence, such as having the power to shape opinions.

Conclusion

Let's hit the rewind button for a second. We've covered the A to Z of being an influencer, right from the basics to the deep dives. Here are some of the takeaways from our discussions

- Choosing a niche isn't just about what's popular; it's about passion.

- Money-making is possible, whether it's through ads, sponsorships, merch sales, affiliate sales, subscriptions, or tips from your fans.

- Community building is crucial. Social media isn't just for selfies; it's a tool to build a loyal community and keep them engaged.

- We talked about consistency with the content calendar and even had a glimpse of what the future holds.

Change is the only constant!

The influencer world isn't static; it's ever-changing. Remember that what's hot today might be yesterday's news tomorrow. The key is to stay adaptable and never stop learning.